THE ART
OF BEING

Single

LIVE A LIFE YOU LOVE

CANDI WILLIAMS

summersdale

THE ART OF BEING SINGLE

An Hachette UK Company
www.hachette.co.uk

Summersdale Publishers Ltd
Part of Octopus Publishing Group Limited
Carmelite House
50 Victoria Embankment
LONDON
EC4Y 0DZ
UK

www.summersdale.com

Printed and bound in Malta

ISBN: 978-1-78685-962-4

Substantial discounts on bulk quantities of Summersdale books are available to corporations, professional associations and other organisations. For details contact general enquiries: telephone: +44 (0) 1243 771107 or email: enquiries@summersdale.com.

♥ CONTENTS

To all the incredible single ladies in my life,
May this little book serve as a constant reminder of how wholeheartedly beautiful, fiercely strong and effortlessly independent you are – and that no partner whatsoever is needed to validate that.

Also, to every single person who is bored of:

- 🤍 Mindlessly swiping left.
- 🤍 Having to answer tedious questions about their non-existent love life.
- 🤍 Pitying looks when they say they're not dating.

I hope this gives you some food for thought, a reminder that you're wonderful just as you are and helps you love yourself even more.

Finally,
To all of those who have seen the light (well, the red flags) and had the courage to leave an emotionally abusive relationship. Yass, queens. High-five to realising your worth.

This one is for all of you.
I hope you enjoy it.
x

INTRODUCTION

Hello, super singleton.

If you're reading this, it's possible that you're already au fait with being single and used to the ups, downs and tedious 'why/how are you still single?' or 'met anyone yet?' questions it brings.

I sure as hell know I am.

Well, this isn't one of those books that preaches to you how to style your hair or what to wear to woo your perfect catch. Nor is it going to tell you how to plan a pity party to mourn past relationships over a lasagne and bottle of Shiraz for one.

Because this book is all about *you* and *your life*.

And if you take one thing from it, let it be this: there is no relationship more important than the one you have with yourself.

Get that right and you'll never go far wrong.

Single equals unique, not alone

'Single', by its very definition, means individual.

Unattached. Exceptional. Unique.

Nowhere under the word 'single' in the dictionary does it state 'a lesser half who needs a better half to complete her/him'.

Because you, right now, exactly as you are, are whole. You are complete.

You are enough.

(I'll keep reminding you of that throughout the book, but don't go forgetting it.)

single

adjective

only one; not one of several.

THE SINGLE SUPERPOWER

For years, we've been sold romantic ideals – through history, the media, marketing and everything in between. Queens who dote dutifully on their kings. Endless ads showing sweet-smiling, glossy couples wandering around sofa shops with love-struck eyes. Articles that tell us how to preen ourselves to be what our potential partner wants.

I'm here to tell you that single is *not* a dirty word.

Being single is *not* something you have to explain, justify or be glum about.

In fact, it has the potential to be one of the most powerful, valuable and enlightening experiences of your life.

Single isn't
a dirty word

More and more people today are choosing to be single.
They are choosing to focus on themselves.
That is their choice.

And who said you can't choose to be single *and* happy?
Single *and* loved.
Single *and* confident.
Single *and* successful.

You don't need a partner to define your happiness, beauty or worth.
   You have everything you need to do that all by yourself.

YOUR STORY

It's time to start focusing on the wonder of you and your story.

On all the amazing things you are, have and love right now.

And the things you want to achieve next.

On being amazingly, unapologetically single.

Time to stop beating yourself up and start living a life you love.

CHAPTER I:

IT'S ALL
About You

Repeat after me:

> *I am enough.*
> *I am complete.*
> *I am unique.*

The truth is, being single is what you make of it. If you treat it like a defect, it'll feel like one. If you embrace all the great things about it and use it as an opportunity to focus on you, you'll reap the benefits.

This little chapter is all about you. Within it, you'll find top tips to help you prioritise yourself and your happiness, and overcome FOBS (Fear Of Being Single).

Why being single matters

So let's start as we mean to go on, with a snapshot of the reasons why being single is one of the most important chapters in your story.

It's time for you to discover your focus

In the spirit of the Spice Girls, what do you want? What do you really, really want?

Beneath it all, what matters to you?

Rank out of ten how satisfied you are with each of these areas of your life right now:

- ♥ Family and friends
- ♥ Career
- ♥ Fitness and physical health
- ♥ Mental health and emotional well-being
- ♥ Money
- ♥ Fun
- ♥ Social life
- ♥ Learning and personal growth

Now pick the areas that you've ranked the lowest. These are your *focus areas* for the coming months. Think about how you can improve your scores in these areas. Throughout the book, you'll find stacks of ideas to help.

You have the space to feel and the time to reflect

When you're in a relationship, you can spend so much of your time with someone else that you rarely get space to think about your emotions – let alone truly feel them. Being on your own gives you that all-important time to reflect on what you want.

You're already full of greatness

If you're living in the hope that a relationship will be the key to your happiness or the missing part of your puzzle, you're misdirecting your energy.

You don't need a knight to rescue you. You're not locked in a turret.

You don't need to find 'the one' to enjoy your life, thrive and have fun.

Finding someone you love may – or may not – be the cherry on the cake for you. But it is not the whole cake – and cakes without cherries are still 100 per cent delicious.

It's a chance to live in the here and now

Spending your time looking back through rose-tinted glasses won't change the past. And, unless you're Mystic Meg, you can't predict what the future holds. But you are totally in charge of your actions and attitude today.

So, your mission, should you choose to accept it, is to worry less about the past – it's gone. Don't panic about the future – it hasn't happened yet. Make the most of how you show up in the here and now – it can make all the difference.

You'll miss single time when it's gone

Honestly, if one day you end up with your wardrobe space squished in half or smelly socks that aren't yours at the bottom of your bed, you'll probably look back on your single life fondly. So don't wish it away – fall in love with it instead.

FACE YOUR FEARS WITH YOUR
FAIRY SOLEMOTHER

What's bugging you? What scares you most about being single? Facing up to your fears has been proved to help you overcome them. So, here are some sprinkles of wisdom from our Fairy Solemother to help you dispel single worries and live your best life – fearlessly.

Ask Fairy Solemother

Fear: *I'm worried I'll never find anyone and that I'll be alone for ever.*

Wisdom: Statistically that's very unlikely. After all, there are 7.5 billion people on this earth, sweetie. And *you* are a catch.

Fear: *I'm happy being single but I want to have kids – and I need a 'significant other' for that.*

Wisdom: False! This is the twenty-first century, darling. There are more options than ever before for becoming a single parent. So, no matter what happens, don't let being single get in the way of your dreams.

Fear: *Where's my happily ever after? I just want to settle down and get married but feel like it'll never happen at this rate!*

Wisdom: I'm going to be real with you for a second here… Marriage can be great but it doesn't automatically equal happily ever after. In fact, lots of married people feel lonely and have their own problems. What will be will be, so live for the now and try not to pin too much on a fairy-tale dress and big, expensive day just because it's what other people are doing. There are so many other beautiful reasons to be happy.

Fear: *I'm sick of feeling like I'll never be good enough for anyone.*

Wisdom: Hell no, honey. Look at your life! You are already good enough – for your friends, your family and all of the other people who adore you. If you feel like you have to change to be 'good enough' for someone else, they're not worthy of you and your special powers. You should never have to reinvent yourself to meet someone else's idea of 'good'. And if you do, you'll probably never feel good enough because you won't be living your truth.

Be yourself, authentically, and let the ones who are worthy love you for you.

Single affirmations

Our brains are amazingly clever but they can't always differentiate between reality and what's only in our heads. When we think something, a mini episode of it happening plays out in our minds, hence why thoughts can feel so real and overwhelming.

This means that the more we think things like 'I hate being single', the more negative thought patterns cement themselves in our brains – and we start to believe them. Thankfully, practising positive affirmations can reduce negative thinking by reprogramming our minds with kinder, more balanced thoughts. Psychologists have been raving about the power of affirmations for years and they're proven to boost our self-esteem and mindset.

These positive affirmations are designed especially for single living. Repeat them daily in your head – or in the mirror for maximum effect.

I don't need to be in a relationship to make myself happy. I can do that all by myself.

I am a strong, beautiful, independent person with my whole future ahead of me.

I choose me. I am my priority.

I will make the most of each day and live my life to the fullest.

Being single does not make me an incomplete or lesser person. I am whole.

I would rather be single than in an unhappy relationship.

I feel more in charge of my life with each day.

Every day is a new adventure. I'm not defined by my past.

I know my worth.

I won't settle just for the sake of it.

I am strong. I am resilient. I am a survivor.

I don't compare myself to others because I'm living my truth.

Don't put your life on
hold waiting for love.

Mandy Hale

THE JOYS OF
being single

JOY #1: *bed bliss*

Yeah sure, spooning's great but have you ever woken up in snoozy starfish bliss with no one else's limbs digging into you?

This is the time to make the most of the bed space being *all yours*. Embrace not having to battle for the best side or the extra pillow, and not waking up teetering on the edge of the bed/floor apocalypse.

Own it. Enjoy every inch. Starfish wide and starfish with pride – you're the bed boss.

WORRY LESS, LOVE YOURSELF MORE

Let's get a few things straight.

Being single doesn't mean you're not worthy of love. It doesn't mean that there's anything wrong with you. And it doesn't mean you have to spend every evening swiping away for Mr or Mrs Right.

We live in a world obsessed with labels and putting people into boxes. But you don't have to justify your singleness to anyone – in the same way that people don't have to justify why they're married or in a relationship.

Instead, choose yourself as a priority and start to love yourself with all the effort and care you would put into a relationship with a significant other.

Be shamelessly single.

You'll thank yourself for it.

FOUR REASONS NOT TO WORRY ABOUT BEING SINGLE

1. Fairy tales aren't real (sorry)

Now, don't get me wrong: I love a love story as much as the next person. But let's not forget Romeo and Juliet's fate or that Cinderella is essentially looking for a man to rescue her from a life of unpaid labour and abusive family members.

The world is constantly changing and people are constantly proving that you don't need an 'other half' to be happy. So be the hero of your own story.

2. People are nosy whatever your relationship status

When you're single, people will probe you about your love life. When you're in a relationship, they'll ask when you're getting married. When you're married, they'll be stroking your tummy enquiring when you're having kids. Laugh and don't let it get to you. Also see our stock answers on pages 148–152 to help you out with prying questions.

3. No one's love is more important than your own

Take it from someone who spent years trying to make up for a lack of self-love with the love of others – it doesn't work. Someone else's love or attention won't make all your problems go away or your dreams come true overnight. Nor will it fix how you feel about yourself. Work on yourself. I know it's hard but it's worth it. Promise.

4. You don't have to be dating to have a good time

Dates can be fun, of course, but so can putting on a new lippy and going for cocktails and giggles with your best mates. There's no need to think that you need a partner to make your life better or more enjoyable – because you can do that all by yourself.

Me Dates

MOVIE NIGHT DELIGHT

That film you've been wanting to see for a while? Go and watch it – all by yourself. Treat yourself to a fancy seat and an XL tub of popcorn and embrace not having to compromise on your choice of film. And if the date goes well, make it a regular thing.

THE JOYS OF
being single

JOY #2: *deep conditioning, all wrapped up*

Being single means more time for self-love. Hooray! So perfect your 'sorry, I'm washing my hair' routine with this pamper-night tip.

Firstly, wash and rinse out your hair as normal. Then, lather on the conditioner (don't be shy – get it all over those ends). Now for the best bit: wrap your hair in a scarf, a recycled plastic bag or something equally ingenious and leave it to soak in for at least an hour before washing out. Trust me, your locks will love you for it.

PS the whole experience is even dreamier if, while your hair is all wrapped up, you strut your stuff around your room like the total legend you are.

Some people said,
'Oh. You don't want to be
alone.' And I said, 'I'm
not alone! I'm with myself.
And myself is fabulous.'

EVA LONGORIA

LEARN TO LOVE YOUR OWN COMPANY

Distractions, distractions, distractions. Our days are full of them. We fill silences with TV, music or chatter. We tap on our phones to avoid sitting with our thoughts. As a generation, we've become pretty good at *doing* stuff, but many of us go to great lengths to avoid just *being*.

The thing with spending time alone is that it gives us a chance to zoom in on ourselves; to understand what we're really thinking and how we're really feeling. What's our inner voice saying and why? When we're not scrolling on social media, what do we actually enjoy doing? Having me time is very important for self-development, so here are some tips for getting over FOBA (Fear Of Being Alone) and enjoying your own company.

1. Make your home somewhere you enjoy being

Spending time alone is often easier when you have a space that you like being in. So, add some little touches to make your room more Zen – candles, fresh flowers and essential oils can be dreamy for this. Alternatively, add some artwork or a rug in your favourite colours to give your senses some love.

2. Have some daily disconnect time

Set some time aside each day to switch off from all distractions – phone off, TV off, tablet banished. What you do in that time is up to you. Write in your journal, meditate, take a bath, go for a walk… Do whatever you fancy – without interruptions.

3. Add some yoga to your life

Yoga is all about practising the art of stillness, making it a wholesome way to spend some time on your own. If it's your first time and you're nervous about going to studio classes, you'll find loads of yoga practices to try online. Just grab yourself a mat and namaste!

4. Get some feel-good food in

Herbal teas, gorgeous juices, healthy snacks – pick up some of the things you love to help make time spent alone that bit tastier! Oh, and treat yourself to 'the nice plates and mugs' – you deserve it!

5. Find your routine

I realised the importance of time and space when I started setting myself a weekend morning routine, where I'd go and sit for half an hour in my favourite coffee shop after the gym and yoga. Getting up earlier and having that time alone became so important for my mental health. Whether it's creative, fitness related or something else, find a way of doing something that makes your soul happy – and make a routine of it.

Five reasons you're amazing (just as you are)

1. There's no one else like you

No one else has your laugh, your eyes, your unique personality – and no one else has lived your story. Your uniqueness is your superpower.

2. You're doing the best you can

You may not have it all figured out right now – but, really, who does? The most important thing is that you're doing your best. So, be gentle with yourself.

3. You're facing your fears

The sheer fact that you're reading this book shows that you're working on yourself. You want to live a life you love and you're taking the action to do that. Go, you!

4. You do great things

From the little things you do for your friends and family
to the big things you've achieved and overcome, you
do things that make people's lives and your own life
better. Never forget that.

5. You're not beholden to anyone

You are free. You are your own person – and you're
no one's fool. You're living your own life, your way.
And that's something to be excited about.

THE JOYS OF
being single

JOY #3: *unashamedly not sharing meal deals*

One of the very, very best things about being single? Not having to share those 'dine in for two' deals. Because, let's be honest, the suggested serving sizes are pretty ambitious – serves two? *Pfft!* Savour every delicious mouthful.

THE ART OF LETTING GO

We don't tend to fall into a perfect single life overnight. In reality, to allow ourselves to live fulfilled lives we often need to let go of things that are weighing us down or halting our progress.

After a break-up or loss, we often clutch on to an idealistic view of 'how things used to be', looking through rose-tinted glasses rather than a realistic, balanced viewpoint. Shifting from being hung up on the past to making peace with the present is key to establishing what you want from life now – and where you want to go next.

Here are five steps to help you master the art of letting go.

1. How are you really feeling?

If you've been through something tough, don't feel you need to put on a brave face. An important first step is to acknowledge how you're really feeling about it. Sad? Angry? Content? Relieved? Write down your thoughts and emotions, and when your friends ask, don't feel you have to hide behind a faux 'I'm fine' response. Be honest.

2. Cry when you need to

Having a cry isn't a sign that you're weak or not coping – it's a sign that you're a real human with real emotions and feelings who's been through a lot. So let it out whenever you need to, and allow yourself to heal.

3. Know that there's no right or wrong way to handle a break-up

After experiencing loss or hard times, focus on what *you* need. Don't force yourself to keep up appearances or do what's 'expected'. Only you will know how you feel, so focus on doing more of what feels good for your heart and mind and less of what you think you 'should' be doing.

4. What are the silver linings here?

Most clouds bring silver linings, and most problems bring lessons and opportunities. For instance, if you've just gone through a break-up, you now have an opportunity to focus on what you want to do next. What wasn't working? What would you like to be different next time?

It's natural to think about the downsides of change but trying to spot the positives will help how you feel and how you grow.

5. Remember: it's not the end

See setbacks as hurdles — not the finish line. They're just things you need to overcome to continue on your path ahead. So, don't ever think that things are 'over' for you — because your future has heaps of exciting potential. In all the years that we're alive, it's unlikely that good things will only happen to us once. Also, how many times have you already been able to look back and laugh at things that you previously cried about? Cry, frown, scream if you need to, but don't give up on hope. You got this.

CHAPTER 2:

LIVING A LIFE
You Love

LIVE LIFE FULFILLED

Living your best life can conjure up hashtagged pictures of Dubai beaches or swanky rooftop bars. But that's really not what it's all about.

A fulfilled life doesn't mean a busier life or doing it for the 'gram. It means focusing on creating a well-rounded life that makes you happy.

All too often it can feel like we're plodding along, drowning in the day-to-day or trying to tick off a never ending to-do list.

But what matters most to you? What makes your soul smile?

This chapter is all about embracing those things and living a life you love.

When you're in love, or dating someone, you filter your life decisions through their eyes. When you spend a few years being who you are, completely unbiased, you can figure out what you actually want.

Taylor Swift

Be more selfish

If, like me, you spend a lot of your time trying to make sure that others are OK then just the thought of 'being more selfish' can be daunting. But putting yourself first a little more often is a vital part of your well-being.

Not sure where to begin? Here's a self-love starter kit.

1. Do less of what you dislike

Sounds obvious, right? But how many times do you find yourself caught up in activities or conversations that you have no genuine interest in?

Think about it this way: every hour you invest in something you don't want to be doing is an hour that could be spent doing something you love.

Find the things that help you grow, make you happy or improve your inner peace – and do more of them.

2. Surround yourself with people who are good for your mental health

In life, you get people who are drains and people who are radiators – those who drain your energy and those who make you feel warm and happy inside. Pick who you spend your time with wisely.

And remember that it is absolutely OK to politely wave goodbye to relationships that no longer make you feel good. It's about give and take, after all.

3. Stop expecting too much of yourself

What's the worst thing that will happen if you don't complete absolutely everything on your to-do list today? Will the world end? Will a flash mob arrive at your door to heckle you? I think not.

Categorise your plans and to-do list into 'super important', 'nice to do' and 'can wait'. You're not a robot, so focus on achieving only what's realistic and congratulate yourself when you do!

4. Schedule some time for you

Sometimes our diaries can end up so back to back with people to see and things to do that we end up completely neglecting number one. You know how it is when you get to the end of the week and feel like you've barely had a moment to yourself? Change that and block out at least a few hours in your diary for some me time.

You might use that to take yourself for a coffee, to have a night of self-love pampering or just to lie in a little longer. You can spend it however you want – the most important thing is that it's time dedicated to you. Enjoy it!

5. See self-improvement as an investment

Learning doesn't have to stop when school, college or university does. Self-improvement can give you the foundations you need to be the best version of yourself.

And I'm not just talking about reading books on other people's success stories. How you approach self-improvement will be totally personal to you. For some, it could be working on physical fitness or flexibility. For others, it could be learning a new skill or trying a talking therapy.

The options are, quite literally, endless. So learn something new – and see it as an investment in yourself, your growth and your relationships.

6. Get more sleep

Honestly, sleep is your bae. Aside from being a dreamy way to wind down, getting a good night's sleep is proven to help boost your mood, mindset and concentration. Here are some top tips for getting a good kip.

- ♥ Aim for 7–8 hours of sleep a night.
- ♥ Put your phone down at least half an hour before going to bed – not only can tech become a mega distraction but the blue light can also really affect your sleep.
- ♥ If you struggle to drift off then try meditation recordings designed to help you fall asleep – there are lots of great free ones online.
- ♥ Make your bedroom sensationally peaceful – try a diffuser, a pillow spray or candles with lavender and geranium in.
- ♥ Get cosy. Fave pyjamas? Tick. Super-comfy sleeping position? Tick. Plumped-up pillows? Double tick.

Me Dates

GET YOUR PAMPER ON

Nothing says self-love like a good bit of pampering. Scour the interweb for fab deals on massages, pedicures and other indulgent treatments.

If you're on a budget, bring the spa experience to your home. Make a facial for under a fiver by mixing together two tablespoons of honey, half a mashed ripe avocado and a squeeze of lemon juice. You can use the mixture on your face and your hair. Leave it on for up to half an hour and say hello to your new glow.

THE SCIENCE
OF BEING SINGLE

Research shows that being single can be genuinely good for your health and well-being. Hooray! And I'm not just talking about having a lower risk of catching coughs, colds and other nasties by kissing and sharing saliva. Here are some psychology-based insights on the benefits of being a super singleton.

1. More time alone = a more rounded personality

It's true: studies have found that having more time alone helps you grow as an individual and that it's linked to an increased sense of freedom and higher levels of creativity and intimacy. Psychologists say that it boosts productivity too – so get ticking off that to-do list.

2. Single people have stronger social networks

As humans we crave closeness. We're wired to connect and social interactions are super important to our well-being. That's another big tick for being single – it gives you more time to socialise and build strong social networks. Experts have found that this can lead to being more resilient too. *Muscly arm emoji*

3. You're smarter with money

It may not feel like it when your online shopping baskets outweigh your bank balance, but a study by Debt.com found that single people tend to have less credit-card debt than married couples. If that's not a perfect excuse to buy a happy-hour cocktail on your debit card, I don't know what is.

4. Less mattress hogging = better sleeping

No big spoon? No worries. An Amerisleep survey found that single people sleep better than people in relationships. It's amazing what not having to fight for the duvet can do for your shut-eye. Oh, and if you're missing snuggles, just google 'body pillow'. You're welcome.

5. Single people are epic problem solvers

When the going gets tough, singletons get solving. Single people have a problem-solving prowess that comes from handling challenges alone (or with a little help from friends or family). This is proven to make you more self-sufficient and calmer under pressure.

If you need a helping hand when times are tricky, try the Don't Panic exercise on the next pages.

Stress-free single living

The Don't Panic exercise (for use in stressful times)

1. Breathe

You can't solve any stressful situation when your body is in stress mode. To get you back into a relaxed and productive state of mind, use the 4-7-8 breathing technique.

> *Firstly, open your mouth and exhale completely with a whooshing sound. Make sure you let it all out.*
>
> *Next, inhale through your nose for the count of four.*
>
> *Then hold your breath for seven counts.*
>
> *Finally, release it all by exhaling from your mouth for eight counts.*

2. Work out what you can control

All too often we get stressed out about things we can't control, like what other people think about us. The reality is that we have no control over many things in life, but we can almost always control our *reactions* to certain situations, our *effort* and our *attitude*.

When you're facing a challenge or something's gone wrong, take a pause to stop and think before you react.

3. Ask yourself:

♥ **What things do I have control over right now?** What can you change or do to help? Which of these do you want to invest your energy into?

♥ **What can I influence right now?** Some things may be out of your control but you may be able to influence them. Think about how you show up to do this. Be calm, pragmatic and clear, and focus on influencing the situation through positive behaviour.

♥ **What am I most scared of?** What's worrying you most? Write these things down and determine which ones you have control or influence over. The ones you can't control or influence should be put aside so you can focus on the others.

♥ **What am I going to do next?** With all of that in mind, write down three actions that you're going to take to address the situation. You can't control or fix everything, but working on the things you can realistically change is much more productive than worrying endlessly about things you can't.

I don't need marriage.
I don't need anyone to
take care of all my needs
and desires. I can take
care of them myself now.

MINDY KALING

WHAT MAKES YOU
TRULY HAPPY?

Having solo time to focus on you is great but where to begin? Start by thinking about what you want in life. What makes you happy? Not just the material things – the rose-gold Range Rover and a flurry of pugs perhaps – but the things you really value, the things that boost your inner peace. Use these three handy coaching questions to help you focus on making positive steps in your super solo life.

1. What do you enjoy and what drains you?

With the seemingly never-ending to-do lists of everyday life, it's easy to end up on autopilot or going through the motions. Take a moment to think about the typical activities you do on a daily basis – which of them do you *enjoy* and which of them *drain* you? This will help you notice what's sucking up your energy and having a negative effect on your well-being and what's boosting it – so you can do more of the stuff that makes you feel good.

2. What does success look like to you?

Everyone's definition of success will be different. Have a think about what success looks and feels like to you. Try to focus on the things that you can control – David Beckham riding into your life on horseback probably isn't one of them, but following your passion and achieving that goal you've always dreamed of could well be.

3. What's the first step you can take to boost your inner happiness and success?

So, now you have a good idea of what happiness and success look and feel like to you. What one thing can you do or change now to move towards that vision? It can be overwhelming to think of the bigger picture sometimes so start small. Think of a positive action or change you can make in the next week. Write it down somewhere you can't miss and make it happen!

Shiny self-improvement ideas

Create your vision board

What do you want from life? How do you want to feel? Capture it all in your own creative vision board – whether a physical or mental one – and make it a constant reminder of your goals and ambitions.

♥ **Meditate more:** add some meditation into your days. Start off with a 3-minute mindfulness recording and work your way up to 10 minutes – you'll feel the benefits!

♥ **Take note:** start a journal to keep track of your thoughts and feelings – and see progress over time.

♥ **Keep fit:** not just for the physical benefits but for the undeniable mental health and well-being benefits too.

♥ **Get your nutrients:** get to know your omega-3 from your vitamin D and see how a little natural boost can help you.

- ♥ **Challenge yourself:** what is that one thing you've always wanted to learn or achieve? Run a marathon? Do one of those super-cool pole-dancing spins? Set yourself a challenge and smash it.

- ♥ **Get on top of your finances:** make the most of your money with one of the many apps designed to help you do exactly that.

- ♥ **Find a mentor:** go for a coffee with someone who inspires you – and pick their brains about the things you're interested in.

- ♥ **Trade TV time for podcasts:** swap out some of your TV time for podcasts or TED Talks – you might surprise yourself with what you learn.

- ♥ **Read outside your comfort zone:** let the wonderful world of reading help you to achieve your goals. See the Further Reading and Resources list on page 156 for self-improvement book suggestions.

- ♥ **Reflect on your learning:** what have you learnt this past week, month and year? It's easy to let self-improvement flow by if you don't take time to reflect.

THE JOYS OF

being single

JOY #4: *working out what matters to you*

Relationships are all about compromise. Being single, on the other hand, gives you some headspace to work out who you are and what you want out of life. Ultimately, you are the most important person in your world. Use your time alone to figure out your focus and work on your own story – at your own pace.

We are complete with or without
a mate, with or without a child.
We get to decide for ourselves
what is beautiful when it comes
to our bodies. That decision
is ours and ours alone.

Jennifer Aniston

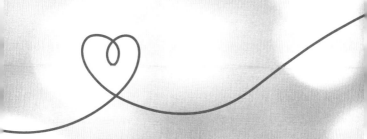

CULTURE AND CREATIVITY

Getting creative or doing something cultural is a great way to spend time alone or with friends when you're single. These mini challenges should help give you a bit of inspiration.

Get theatrical

- ☑ Turn up at the theatre on the night and watch whatever performance is showing.
- ☑ Volunteer in the box office of a local theatre – you normally get to stay and watch the show for free.
- ☑ Offer to help with costumes or make-up for an independent performance.
- ☑ Fancy yourself as a bit of a thespian? Join the local am-dram group.
- ☑ Grab a theatre programme and book tickets to at least one play of your choice.

Get arty

- ☑ Join a craft or drawing group in your local community.
- ☑ Make your own beauty oil blends or other craft goodies, and surprise your family and friends with them.
- ☑ Offer to run a craft event for a local Brownies or Scouts group.
- ☑ Work your creative magic to make the window of a local charity shop wow passers-by.
- ☑ Take a photography class to brush up on what makes a perfect snap.
- ☑ Take a life drawing class – purely for artistic reasons, obviously…
- ☑ Buy some fresh flowers or pick some wild ones, arrange them beautifully and take them into a care home to brighten up the residents' day.
- ☑ Make some birthday, thank-you or Christmas cards and sell them to raise money.

Get musical

- ☑ Explore different open mic nights and download the tracks of any artists you love.

- ☑ Learn that instrument you've always fancied playing. You'll find that some places do beginners' lessons, where everyone's in the same boat.

- ☑ Join a choir. Honestly, joining an R 'n' B choir was one of the best single decisions I've made – it's a great way to meet new people and singing totally soothes the soul.

- ☑ Go to a gig on your own – and dance and sing like no one's watching.

- ☑ Who have you always wanted to see live? List five artists or bands, check when they're touring and try to see as many of them as you can.

- ☑ Go to a festival, let your hair down (literally) and meet some awesome new people.

Get learning

- ☑ Visit three local museums you've never been to before.
- ☑ Start learning a new language, because you never know when you'll need to say 'Hi, I'm single' or 'Mine's a G & T' abroad.
- ☑ Master modern calligraphy – it looks great in cards and you'll wow your pals.
- ☑ Teach yourself to cook an authentic meal from one of your favourite countries. Mac 'n' cheese doesn't count – sorry!

Get fit

☑ Know your HIIS from your HIIT, and your PiYo from your Hot Flow? Give an exercise class you've never ever done before a go – it might just become your new fave.

☑ Pick up the pace with the 300,000-step monthly challenge. Aim for 10,000 steps a day and see if you can hit 300,000 steps by the end of the month.

☑ Mix up your workout game! If you normally default to cardio, try some strength training – and vice versa. YouTube is a great starting place for inspiration.

☑ Prep a healthy lunch the night before work to avoid falling into the 'meal deal' trap, saving yourself pennies and calories.

☑ Aim for 2.5 hours of moderate exercise (like walking or swimming) or 1.5 hours of vigorous exercise (such as running, spinning or circuits) a week. See how many weeks you can keep it up for.

Me Dates

PHONE-FREE CAKE DATE

Leave your phone at home and take yourself out for coffee and cake. Find somewhere that does irresistible sweet treats, pick the one that catches your eye and savour every last mouthful. Sit. People-watch. Read. Enjoy some me time, and give your thumb and mind a break from the daily scroll. Civilisation survived pre-Wi-Fi connections, so I'm sure an hour without it won't hurt.

Community vibes

Make the most of what's all around you.

Embracing what your local area has to offer is a great way to spend some solo time and to get to know new people.

1. Pop to your local on your own

That's what public houses are for, after all. If you fancy a drink and some company, don't feel like you need to wait on friends to pop to your local pub or bar. And, who knows, you might just get chatting to someone new.

2. Spend some time with people in need

From board games with elderly people in care homes to helping put on an event, there are always people and places in the community in need of a bit of support. It'll make you feel good inside and it's a really positive way to spend a few hours.

3. Serve up a hearty dinner at a homeless shelter or food bank

Food banks and homeless shelters are amazing places. Why not contact a few to see how you can help? Putting together 'care packages' for homeless people or serving up soup is a great activity to do alone or with friends.

4. Love animals? Start dog walking

Dog walking is an awesome way to keep fit and meet fellow animal lovers. If you don't have a dog of your own, try uploading a post in a local group to offer your dog-walking skills.

5. Volunteer in a charity shop

Charity shops rely on volunteers so they're almost always looking for extra pairs of hands. It's a chance to do good *and* seek out some stylish bargains.

6. Shop independent

Get to know your nearby independent stores. You'll be supporting the community's small businesses while meeting new people *and* discovering some local treats. Start off by going for a walk, seeing how many independent shops you can spot in your neighbourhood and making a conscious effort to go in and find out more about them.

7. Check out your local political parties

Make your voice heard on what's happening and being discussed in your area. Because, let's be honest, politics has never needed strong, smart, awesome people more than it does right now.

8. Host your own event

Why not put on your own event in the local community space? It's a creative way to meet people and do something positive for your hood. Here are a few ideas to start you off:

- ☑ Charity coffee and cake morning
- ☑ Craft day for all ages
- ☑ Community quiz night
- ☑ Super street party
- ☑ Jumble sale or clothes swap
- ☑ Charity car-wash day

Being alone is just as
important as being
in any relationship.
That's an opportunity
to learn and grow.

CHIDERA EGGERUE

THE JOYS OF
being single

JOY #5: *time to heal your heart and mind*

I'm not talking about healing in a Marvin Gaye way here. But being single gives you time to focus on your emotional well-being and heal any unresolved issues. Mindfulness, yoga, talking therapies and journaling – they're all great ways to calm your mind, soothe your soul and find your inner joy.

Me Dates

PODCAST PICNIC

Download a new podcast, audiobook or TED Talk, pack yourself a picnic of all your favourite foods and take yourself to the park for a date. There are so many inspirational podcasts and talks popping up every day. Add snacks and a sunny day to the occasion and you're onto a winner.

CHAPTER 3:

ADVENTURES IN
Singledom

LET THE ADVENTURES BEGIN

New people, new places, new experiences – it's all part of life's journey.

And being single is the perfect time to explore and adventure; to break free of monotony and try awesome things you've never done before.

From small steps to big jaunts, you'll find adventurous ideas for every budget in this chapter.

So roam free, broaden your horizons and make some unforgettable new memories along the way.

Say yes more

Do you automatically talk yourself out of things when you see something cool advertised or someone invites you to an event? Coming up with excuses in your mind, like:

It's a bit expensive though...

Who will feed the dog?

What if I don't know anyone and everyone else is bezzies?

What if we stopped thinking about all the things that could go wrong and started thinking about all the things that could go right? Like...

Finding your passion

Meeting new friends for life

Making unforgettable memories

Having those eureka life-changing moments

When it comes to trying new things, what have you really got to lose? Because you've got a whole lot to gain.

So, start saying yes more. And here's to fun adventures!

adventure

noun

an unusual and exciting or
daring experience.

DO SOMETHING DIFFERENT

Forget the same old, same old. Open your mind to the exciting and the new. Here are some ideas to help you take chances, broaden your horizons and discover new things that you'll love.

Start small with a microadventure

Not ready to go all out with a big adventure yet? Try a microadventure – an adventure that is 'small and achievable, for normal people with real lives'. The idea was created by British adventurer Alastair Humphreys, who firmly believes you don't have to hang-glide the highest mountains, drain your savings or parachute in Peru to have an incredible adventure, as adventure is all around us.

So, what are you waiting for? Start planning your bespoke microadventure – the location and itinerary are up to you. The only rules are that it's short, simple, local and cheap – and fun, of course!

Make the most of the beauty around you

From national parks to the coastline, it's likely that there are plenty of adventure-worthy places to explore not too far from your doorstep – many of which will be free.

Check out the websites of outdoors organisations, as most have geo-searches that show the places and spaces near you. Roam along riversides. Ponder around gorgeously green parks. Get lost in a real-life secret garden. Go for a relaxing beach walk and find the most beautiful shell you can.

Make it mindful, taking in all the sights and smells. And don't forget to take some snaps – for the memories, not just the 'gram.

Learn to catch waves

Surfing doesn't just look super cool but it's a skill you can use all around the world. So if you haven't already, why not try a few surfing lessons? Beautiful beaches, sunny skies, crystal-clear waters – what's not to love?

You can do it at home or abroad, and there are lots of awesome surf camps for beginners, where you'll learn to catch your first waves and enjoy a luscious beach holiday.

Downward dog on a stand-up paddleboard

As if stand-up paddleboarding along a stunning river or coastline wasn't enough – now you can add flexi-fun yoga moves into the equation. You can take stand-up paddleboarding classes in countless locations across the world – from the UK coast to the beaches of Costa Rica and Canada. Guided by expert teachers, you'll start with the basics and work your way up. And if you lose your footing, you'll have the soothing water to land in rather than a hard floor!

Top tip: balance not your strong point? You might want to start off with a practice class in the pool to align your chakras before you start waving your limbs about on open water!

Volunteer at a festival or event

Meet new people *and* enjoy a glittery, fun event on a budget – what's not to love? Volunteering at a festival or event is an awesome way to inject some excitement into your year without breaking the bank.

You can volunteer for everything from big-name festivals – like Glastonbury and Shambala – to local Prosecco festivals, cheese festivals, food and music events, and many more. Most volunteering opportunities range from selling tickets to bar and charity work, and you'll normally be offered a number of hours or shifts in exchange for a free ticket and food. Win–win.

Retreat yourself

We've spoken a lot about having some me time but
I totally get that it can be hard to find time to do this
when you're caught up in the day-to-day.

   A retreat can be one sure-fire way of guaranteeing
yourself some time and space for rejuvenation.
Whether it's a yoga or mindfulness retreat, a spa
break or a trip focused on self-love, these experiences
can be totally life-changing. So, maybe it's time to
(re)treat your lovely self.

THE JOYS OF
being single

JOY #6: *not feeling guilty*

Do your thing. Stay out until 2 a.m. doing karaoke. Go out with friends three nights in a row. Eat that chocolate cake. Do what *you* want, without the pangs of guilt or worry. This is your time to shine!

Do the thing

You know that thing you've always wanted to do – be it travelling the world, becoming a personal trainer, bungee jumping, getting a tattoo or something totally different – now's the time to just go for it!

Honestly, what's stopping you? There's a quote I love about how in life we only regret the chances we didn't take and the decisions we took too long to make. Don't let that happen to your bucket-list goal. Do your thang, you adventurous single human, you.

Explore five new spots where you live

Adventures don't have to mean big budgets and high mileage – quite the opposite, in fact. A great way to open your eyes to new adventures is to find fresh, exciting things to do in the place you live.

Ignite your adventurous streak by challenging yourself to go to five new different places. These could be independent bars or restaurants, a new fitness class or something completely random. Mark them down and keep note of your faves.

Experience the wonders of wine tasting

A mini adventure that I like to try out anywhere in the world is wine tasting. From checking out sparkling wines to amazing vineyard tours, it's a brilliant way to discover your favourite wines and learn interesting new things about the world's best-loved grape drink. The atmosphere tends to be fun and friendly too – and you'll leave with that warm, fuzzy feeling inside.

Top tip: always keep a note of your favourite wine, so you can track it down and impress your friends next time you have a dinner party.

Hip-hop, meet yoga

Yes, that's right. Hip-hop yoga is a thing – and it's a ridiculously fun, bootylicious thing. Think high-energy yoga flows while getting down low to some epic hip-hop beats. You'll leave feeling rejuvenated and full of life. It's a great way to meet people too.

You can find classes in most big cities, or, for a taster, give it a search on YouTube and groove from the comfort of your front room or bedroom.

Being single is delightfully more than it's cracked up to be.

Chelsea Handler

Adventures around the world

The world is your oyster — make the most of it. If you've got the travelling bug, being single might just be the perfect time to explore some of the gorgeous places this world has to offer. Check out these international adventure ideas for inspiration.

Spa yourself silly in Bali

If you're looking for a big adventure that'll leave you super refreshed, try beautiful Bali. Enjoy the flower baths and yoga, or rid yourself of negative energy and emotional unrest with a traditional Balinese Boreh treatment or Aura Chakra healing. Bliss!

Bike along the river in Bordeaux

Into wine, cheese and laid-back luxury? Then Bordeaux could be right up your adventure alley. Hire a bike, cycle along the river and soak up the views of the world's most famous wine region, then wind down with a glass of Bordeaux – just like every chic solo traveller should. *C'est magnifique.*

Snorkel with turtles

You can swim with super-cute sea turtles in countless destinations across the world. Turtles are known for being calm and ancient-looking, and you can swim with them from just six feet deep in some of the world's clearest, bluest waters. Maybe even plan a trip to catch a glimpse of turtles laying their eggs or of baby turtles hatching on the beach.

Ski your worries away

If you're more into slopes than snorkels, skiing or snowboarding could be an awesome snowy solo adventure for you.

Top tips for making a solo snow trip affordable:

♥ Go in low season (dates outside public holidays and school breaks).

♥ Avoid the most popular destinations – lots of the big-name resorts will have big price tags.

♥ Choose self-catering as it's normally cheaper than catered chalets or hotels.

♥ Canvass your friends to see if they have any skiwear you can borrow – or rent!

Be Scandi cool in Stockholm

From living your best life in stunning, chandelier-lit bars to shimmying to guilty pleasures in the ABBA Museum, super-cool Stockholm has something for every solo traveller to enjoy. It's also known for its low crime rate and very welcoming culture. So if you fancy a little European getaway, don your dark glasses and go enjoy the architecture – and gin.

Go on an African safari

Animal lover? *Lion King* superfan? Why not go wild with a once-in-a-lifetime safari trip? Go on safari with a group of other solo adventurers (if you can't persuade any pals to come with you), or, if you're feeling extra adventurous, you can even train to be a safari guide!

Sip sparkling sangria in Porto

It might be known as 'Lisbon's little sister', but Porto is every bit as cool as the Portuguese capital. It's famous for its port, its sprawling river and incredible culture. Whether you're into exploring the Harry Potter-esque bookshop that inspired J. K. Rowling, eating fresh seafood from local BBQs or visiting funky bars, you won't have a dull moment in this gorgeous city.

PS its sparkling sangria is a total must-try – perfect for sipping riverside.

Book an impromptu trip somewhere totally new

Make the most of the cheap flights on offer and book a thrifty weekend away somewhere you've never been before. Use flight comparison sites to find the dates with the cheapest flights, suss out accommodation options and get it in the diary. You can get to so many ace places in just a couple of hours, so make the most of it!

Top tip: this is a great one for payday! If you're going alone, definitely check out the solo travel top tips over the next few pages.

YOUR ADVENTURE
BUCKET LIST

Inspired but not sure where to start?
Jot down:

- ♥ One destination you want to visit.
- ♥ Two famous landmarks you want to see.
- ♥ Three dishes you want to try.
- ♥ Four words you want to learn in different languages.
- ♥ Five different types of animals that you want to see up close.

Now, go make it happen!

Top tips for travelling solo

Travelling solo might seem daunting but it needn't be. In fact, with the freedom to explore all the things you want and no agenda but your own, it might just be one of the most incredible experiences of your life. Here are some top tips to help you on your way.

1. Avoid the pesky single supplements

Ugh, damn those single supplements. Yep, that's right: some travel companies charge extra for people travelling alone. Luckily, with a bit of clever internet searching, you can find supplement-free options – search for 'single supplement waived' or 'no single supplement' along with your chosen destination. Another tip is to work out how much the single supplement adds to your trip and research cheaper flights and holiday packages to make up for it.

2. Go your own way

Guidebooks are great for inspiration, but give yourself at least one day to adventure with no plan or schedule. Walk. Explore. Swim. Get coffee. Say hi to people. Do exactly what you want to do – what you feel like doing – with no time limit or checklist. Your only mission for the day: enjoy it.

3. Embed yourself in the culture

Embracing a different culture is one of my favourite things about travelling. Treat your taste buds to authentic cuisine and book yourself on to some tours to soak up the sights and learn the lifestyle from the locals.

4. Eat alone – and relish it

Eating out alone is absolutely acceptable in every country. Instead of shying away from it, make the most of it! Ask the waiters for their recommendations. Say yes to that dessert – who's judging? And practise mindful eating by truly savouring every mouthful, thinking about the flavours, the sensations and the smells. *Bon appétit!*

5. Venture out of your comfort zone

Adventures are all about new experiences, so challenge yourself to do something that you wouldn't do at home. Talk to a stranger. Learn a traditional dance. Wear a colour that you'd never normally wear. The options are limitless. For inspiration, check out the different excursions on offer. It's a great way to meet new people too.

6. Stay safe

Always keep family or friends up to date with your plans and whereabouts. Keep your bag and belongings close at all times. And drink safely – when you're having fun and meeting new people, of course you'll want to let your hair down, but stay in control of your alcohol levels to keep yourself safe.

Make sure you have somewhere safe to stay, and familiarise yourself with your surroundings, how to get around and how to get home in every place you visit.

THE JOYS OF
being single

JOY #7: *karaoke for every road trip*

You know the playlist fear you get when you have someone in the passenger seat... What radio station should I put on? What playlist will they like? Is Little Mix acceptable for this occasion? Can I rap along to Kanye without them bursting into fits of laughter?

Forget all of that. Guilt-free music choices for road trips are another perk of single living. So rap away, listen to cheesy radio shows and download that guilty pleasures playlist. Make every journey about karaoke. Do you and own it.

EMBRACE THE #ARTOFBEINGSINGLE PHOTO CHALLENGE

Don't forget to capture your magical solo adventures – it's a great excuse to give your photography skills a boost. Here's a list of fun snaps to capture on your solo travels.

- ♥ Your first stop
- ♥ A selfie of you and a local
- ♥ You doing something you've never done before
- ♥ A famous landmark
- ♥ A souvenir
- ♥ A traditional local dish
- ♥ A skyline photo
- ♥ Your holiday read
- ♥ You chilling out
- ♥ An animal
- ♥ Your last stop

CHAPTER 4:

SINGLE AND READY
to Mingle

THE DATING GAME

Dating today doesn't have to be all swipes and selfies. In fact, it's all about you – and what *you* want to get out of it.

> *If you fancy a flirt, flirt.*
> *If you want to date, date.*
> *If you don't feel ready, don't.*

Date on your terms, as, when and how you like.

Break rules. Text first. Don't settle. Most importantly, enjoy the ride.

This little chapter's all about dating – the good, the bad and the funny.

The new dating mantras

Say goodbye to outdated traditions like 'never be the one to text first', 'don't kiss on the first date', 'men should be the ones to ask women out' and all those other silly rules that glossy magazines and romcoms have imparted on us.

The dating game has changed. You're in charge now. And whether you're looking for 'the one', having some fun or keeping your options open, the single most important thing is that you enjoy yourself and do what's right for you.

So, I've banished the dusty manual of old, unhelpful dating traditions and replaced it with some modern-day mantras. Enjoy!

The first commandment: work out what you want and put that first

The bottom line: you're not dating for anyone but yourself. What is it that you want from dating? To meet new people? A loving relationship? Flirty fun? Unsure? Think about what it is that you'd like from the dating process and keep that at the front of your mind throughout.

The second commandment: *do not* – I repeat, *do not* – entertain a-holes

Life's too short to invest time and energy in people who don't deserve it. Keep an eye out for time-wasters and a-holes. Notice the red flags and if it doesn't feel right to you, stop. Protect yourself and your feelings.

The third commandment:
remember that you do not exist
to stroke anyone's ego

Put yourself first. You're not running an on-call service for when people need attention or their ego stroked. If someone wants to play games, they should go and get a Monopoly board because you, my friend, are much better than that.

The fourth commandment:
don't over-stalk

We've all been there. You're just having a look at their Instagram and, before you know it, you're on their second aunt Janet's holiday photos from 2014. But let's be real: it is very rare that anything good comes from a social-media stalk. You just end up wondering who charly85xoxo is and why she's liking all their pictures. Save yourself the unanswered questions – and the risk of accidentally liking a post that's three years old.

The fifth commandment: stop waiting for them to text

Watching your phone endlessly, checking to see when someone was last online or texting them again – none of these things will make someone text back faster. A person will text back at one time and one time only: when they're ready to.

All the time you're eagerly waiting and hoping, you're putting your happiness in their hands. The real question is: do you want to be with someone who doesn't keep in touch regularly? Are they worth your time? Focus less on what they're doing or why they're not texting back, and more on what you deserve.

The sixth commandment: enjoy dating but don't depend on it

Dating can be a fun part of being single but please don't ever feel like your whole life depends on meeting someone. You don't *need* another half or significant other, because you are whole and significant already. Look for someone who enhances your life, but doesn't own it.

DATING STAGE 1:
MEETING BAES

You're single, free and ready to mingle – as much or as little as *you* choose. If you want to get out there, here are a few top tips for getting in the dating game.

Set yourself a swipe window

Apps are often the first step for meeting people today. If you choose to go down the dating app route, let it become a part of your life but not take it over. Set yourself a swipe window – a daily or weekly slot to focus on dating apps. It'll make it more enjoyable without eating up your me time.

Get out there – literally

Go old school and get out and meet new people face-to-face. Go to your favourite bar, coffee shop or hang out on your own, and don't be afraid to get talking to other people who are on their own. They might well be doing the same thing. Also, try real-life speed dating or a blind date set up by a friend. If it worked for the ladies in *Sex and the City*…

Move beyond the small talk

'Hi. How are you?'
'Good, thanks. You?'
'Nice weekend?'
'Yeah. You?'

I don't know about you but I find that the small chat can soon wear thin. Below are a few icebreakers to spice up your dates a little.

Cats or dogs?

If you were invisible for the day, what's the first thing you'd do?

If you were in Harry Potter, what house would you be in?

If you had your own talk show, who would your first three guests be?

Would you rather live in space or under the sea? And why?

Dating stage 2: enjoying dates

Yes, they can be nerve-wracking but dates should be fun! So, focus on keeping an open mind and enjoying yourself rather than putting pressure on yourself.

Don't panic

You're nervous. It's natural. They will be too. Take some deep breaths and just think of it as having a chat and getting to know a potential new friend.

Do something fun

Grabbing a drink or bite to eat is all well and good, but why not add a bit of excitement to your dates? Crazy golf, pizza making, a comedy night, rock climbing, a board games cafe – get those fun vibes flowing as you get to know each other.

Try not to get too drunk

It's normal to want a drink to calm your nerves when meeting someone for the first time but try not to get too drunk – it makes everything that bit blurrier, including figuring out whether you like them enough to see them again!

Be fully present

Phones down, eyes up. Give every date your full attention and make the most of getting to know each other.

Reflect with a date debrief

Ah, the post-date debrief! Always reflect on your date afterwards and allow yourself some time to think about how it went and if you'd like to see them again.

Here are a few things to consider:

- ♥ How did you feel at the end of the date?
- ♥ What did you like about them?
- ♥ What didn't you like?
- ♥ Did they meet your expectations? Did they exceed them?
- ♥ What is your brain telling you?
- ♥ What is your gut telling you?
- ♥ Would you like to see them again? If so, what would you like to know more about?

DATING STAGE 3: WATCHING OUT FOR RED FLAGS

Early dating should be fun and exciting – with butterflies and belly flutters – but always stay alert to those niggling red flags. Here's just a handful to look out for, but really it's all about trusting your gut and knowing your worth.

Red flag #1: they tell you all their exes are 'crazy' or 'psychos'

Forget anyone who blames an ex for their behaviour or who's looking for a new bae to 'change' or 'fix' them. People are responsible for themselves and changing their own bad behaviour. That is not your job.

Red flag #2: they repeatedly go quiet for a while then pop back up again

If they're playing with your emotions, remember you are not a board game. You deserve better.

Red flag #3: they're flakier than a Mr Whippy with an extra flake

You want someone you can rely on, right? If they cancel and can't stick to plans in these early stages, are they worth you giving up your time for long-term?

Red flag #4: they're glued to their phone

Don't get me wrong, we all love to know what's kicking off in the Twittersphere, but this is the time for you two to get to know each other – that should be the priority, not tapping away on phones.

Red flag #5: they don't put the effort in

If they seem half-hearted or nonchalant about seeing you, the chances are they aren't worthy of your precious time.

Red flag #6: they become overly jealous or possessive of you

Whoa, no. Do you look like a bungalow or semi-detached house? Because from where I'm sitting, you're no one's property. Trust issues so early on are a massive red flag.

Red flag #7: they don't like labels

You know the ones: when you have all the components of a relationship but they don't want to 'put a label on it' or it feels secret. Forget that. Any partner should be proud to shout from the rooftops that they're with you.

Red flag #8: they only text you when it's late or they're drunk

Hey babe xoxo and a string of nonsensical messages at 2.51 a.m. don't constitute a meaningful conversation. We all fall into the drunk text trap now and again but watch out for it becoming a consistent theme.

Red flag #9: they gaslight you and make you doubt yourself

Gaslighting is a form of control when someone deliberately makes you doubt or second-guess yourself. Your gut instinct is a powerful thing, so if someone is constantly making you feel 'overly sensitive', 'paranoid' or 'in the wrong', don't mistake their mind games for the truth.

Red flag #10: they don't respect your boundaries

Pushy behaviour, making you feel guilty for not doing what they want, not taking things at a pace you're comfortable with – these are all major red flags. Anyone who doesn't respect or who belittles your boundaries isn't worthy of a place in your life.

So many people think
being single is the end
of something, but it's
really a beginning – a
good beginning.

LAUREN LONDON

CHAPTER 5:

'SINGLE' DOES NOT
Equal 'Alone'

BEING SINGLE DOESN'T MEAN BEING ALONE

In fact, being single can help heal our mental health whereas being alone can hinder it.

The word 'alone' has negative connotations – it conjures up images of Kevin McCallister and the series of disasters he went through when left home alone.

Being single, however, gives us time to get to know our true selves with the same care and attention that we'd use to get to know a friend or potential partner.

In this chapter, we'll explore ways in which being single can be a nurturing – and far from lonely – experience.

THE JOYS OF
being single

JOY #8: *feeding your friendships*

Well, don't literally feed them (although I am always open to being fed delicious food by friends). Being single is an ideal time to focus more on your friendships. Good friends are there for you through break-ups, make-ups, tears, fears and giggles. They have your back when you need them most. But it's a two-way street, so invest in them, look after them and be sure to show them some love.

What a lovely surprise to
finally discover how unlonely
being alone can be.

Ellen Burstyn

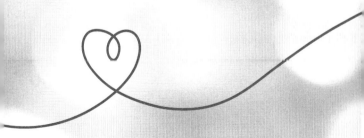

Your support network

Everyone needs a helping hand or shoulder to cry on from time to time.

And as you grow older, you see that it's less about how many people are in your contacts and more about who's there when you need them.

Your true support network. The ones who have your back when it matters.

Think about your support network

Who can you talk to when you need some advice or someone to listen?

Who do you trust with your biggest problems or secrets?

Who's always there?

Who helps you to see the bright side even on the darkest days?

Those are your people.

KEEPING YOUR SUPPORT NETWORK BLOSSOMING

Nurture and nourish

Think of your support network as a garden, where each person in it is a flower. If you don't take the time to check in and give them some attention, they'll wilt.

Now, I'm not suggesting you should go round watering your family and friends. But be consistent, be caring – and your relationships will only grow stronger and more beautiful.

Grow and flourish

Adding new flowers to your garden only makes it richer. As well as tending to your existing support network, stay open to letting worthy new people into your life. Don't be afraid to sow new seeds of friendship – you never know, something amazing could grow from it.

THE JOYS OF
being single

JOY #9: *getting comfy with your own company*

However extroverted or introverted you are, it's always good to learn to enjoy your own company. I'm not talking about sitting in silence and twiddling your thumbs. I'm talking about making the most of me time – whether that's bringing a wholesome new meaning to Netflix and chilling, practising self-care, reading a book or just generally moving yourself out of FOMO zone to 'I kinda like my time alone'.

A little bit of TLC goes a long way

In this busy world we live in, maintaining your support network takes some TLC.

Time

Making time for other people doesn't mean hour-long phone calls every day. A nice text here and there, a little card to surprise someone, making sure you're free for birthdays and important dates, or catching up over coffee are all things that show someone they matter.

Love

They say it makes the world go round and it's definitely at the heart of keeping your support network blooming. Show your network love and the chances are that they'll return the favour when you need it most.

Communication

Communication is so important. Keep in touch with the people that matter to you. Listen to their feelings as well as sharing yours. And if something about the relationship is bothering you, find a way to talk about it. A problem shared is a problem halved.

SHOWING FRIENDSHIPS SOME LOVE

Being single means having more time to invest in your friendships. From F to S, here's a guide for making your friendships flourish.

F is for...

Finding time

The older we get, the busier our schedules seem to be. But to keep friendships blossoming, you need to put in time for togetherness. Literally.

> *Friendship tip: schedule in your next date for a get-together at the end of every catch-up with a pal. That way, you have something fun to look forward to already waiting in the diary and no chance of leaving it too long.*

R is for...

Recognising it's about give and take

It might sound simple but remembering that friendships are all about give and take is key to maintaining healthy relationships.

Sometimes your friend might be going through a hard time and will need to lean on you a little more, and vice versa at other times. The most important thing is that you're there for them and they're there for you.

> *Friendship tip: check in. Ask your friends how they really are and tune in carefully to their response.*

I is for...

Integrity

Real friendships are about a whole lot more than just hanging out in the same circles. Loyalty never, ever goes out of fashion. So, stay true to your true friends. Treat them with the same respect behind their backs that you would to their faces. Love them gently and stand up for them fiercely.

Friendship tip: jot down all the friends you'd consider loyal – and why not drop them a spontaneous text to let them know you love 'em?

E is for...

Embracing each other's flaws

No one's perfect. In my case, I'm nearly always five minutes late and I can be a real sloth at replying to text messages. On the other hand, I'm loyal until the end of time and always there for my friends with a glass of wine or a cuddle when needed.

My point is that every person has flaws. And friendships, like sisterhoods, are all about embracing each other's flaws as well as the good points. After all, you can't enjoy the rainbow without a little rain.

Friendship tip: write down five things you love about your best friends – and get them to do the same. It's good for the soul.

N is for...

Never taking friendships for granted

I see lots of people who get into relationships and stop investing time in their friendships, only to find that they need them again when things go wrong. Don't be that person.

Partners may come and go, but good friendships can be lifelong relationships. Keep putting time and effort into them.

Friendship tip: make sure your friends know you love them – just as you would in a relationship.

D is for...

Don't be jel

Don't compare your life and timeline to your friends'. I know that seeing others hitting milestones in their lives can make you reflect on your situation but it's not a competition. And it doesn't mean that these things won't happen to you (if you want them). Be happy for your friends' happiness and embrace being part of a new chapter in their lives.

Friendship tip: keep having friend time no matter what stage you're at in your lives. Just adapt to the shape of it!

S is for...

Saying sorry

'Sorry' can often feel like the hardest word to say –
but it's definitely one of the most important.

 As human beings, not perfect robots, it's inevitable
that we won't get things right all the time. The most
important thing is being kind and humble enough
to say sorry if we upset someone or hurt their
feelings. Rather than dwell on a bad feeling or worry,
apologise and try to move on.

> *Friendship tip: we can all be stubborn from
> time to time but it's often important to look
> at the bigger picture. If you value a friendship
> and things go wrong, don't be too proud to
> reach out and try to put them right.*

THE JOYS OF
Being Single

JOY #10: *being able to bust out the 'Single Ladies' dance so passionately Bey would be proud*

Being single gives you a damn good opportunity to proudly bust a groove to Beyoncé's ultimate anthem to singledom. So throw your hands up, strut around that dance floor and celebrate being single, sexy and free.

'Oh oh oh, oh oh oh, oh oh oh, oh oh oh…'

Ideas for a super-fun single Valentine's Day

Because who said Valentine's Day was just for couples? *Pfft!*

♥ **Make it Galentine's Day:** grab your single gals, stockpile all the Prosecco, get your face masks on and order the takeaway of all takeaways. Perfect!

♥ **Take a cooking class:** lots of cookery schools offer solo cooking classes on V-Day – a chance to cook up a tasty storm and meet some new single huns.

♥ **Treat yourself to a pressie (or five):** and get some beautiful flowers for your home too. Who said you need a partner to spoil you?

♥ Write a card to all the people you love in your life: let them know why they're special to you on V-Day. Everyone needs a little love, after all.

♥ Valentine's Day, what? treat it like it's any other day – but treat yourself to something nice with the money you've saved on overpriced heart-shaped gimmicks.

♥ Dedicate your evening to self-love: write a list of things you rate about yourself, put on your most empowering songs and dance around in a Minnie Mouse onesie – you do you.

♥ Have a mates' night out: feeling mischievous? Round up the troops and head to your favourite restaurant for a night of giggles and silliness. Make all the tables of two wish they were with you.

FAMILY TIES

You don't owe your family explanations.

You don't owe them grandkids.

In reality, you have nothing to prove to anyone but yourself.

> *'So, when are you going to bring a nice girl/boy home?'*
>
> *'When are you going to give me a grandchild?'*

We've all been there.

But remember that, prying questions aside, your family probably only want what's best for you. Would they really want you to be in an unhappy relationship for the sake of getting married or having kids?

So, don't feel like you have to keep up appearances. Do things in your own time. And be honest – let your loved ones know you're focusing on yourself and your happiness.

> *Top tip: why not use your singledom as a chance to nourish your relationships with your fam?*

And while we're talking about family...

Here's a high-five to the super single parents!
 You inspirational, multitalented human heroes are doing awesomely.
 Keep smashing it.

Me Dates

WINE AND DINE YOURSELF

Eat out alone, fearlessly. And I don't mean a rushed bite to eat, worrying that everyone's watching you (they're not, by the way). I'm talking three delicious courses and a glass of your favourite wine. Try something totally new or stick to your favourite thing on the menu – the main thing is that you cherish your own company and remember that you don't need a partner to do the things you love.

You're one of a kind

Fact: there are lots of like-minded people out there looking to meet and hang out with people like you.

If you don't believe me, just try an app like Meetup that brings people together for events and fun things to do based on their interests. Whatever your age, whether you're into cinema or CrossFit, gin tasting or going to the theatre, there's something for everyone.

There are plenty of similar apps and groups too, and they're a brilliant way to make friends and meet new people – with no pressure on who buys the first round!

THE JOYS OF
being single

JOY #11: *not having to compromise*

Sure, compromises are important, but have you ever binged back to back on an entire series of *your choice* while eating the takeaway *you want* followed by *your favourite* ice cream flavour?

No? Then you haven't lived.

Stop compromising. Start living.

You alone are enough.
You have nothing to
prove to anybody.

MAYA ANGELOU

TACKLING LONELINESS

Loneliness can happen to anyone – old or young, male or female, married or single.

One of the common misconceptions about loneliness is that it's synonymous with being alone. However, you could be in a room full of people and still feel incredibly lonely. Likewise, your social life could be brimming with exciting things, but you can still go home in the evening and feel totally lonely – I know, I've been there.

It's a horrible feeling but one that is absolutely nothing to be ashamed of. So, please don't suffer in silence – here are some pointers to help you understand and tackle loneliness.

Think about what's making you feel lonely

Break-ups, divorces, bereavements, new settings, comparing your life to others' are just some of the things that can trigger feelings of loneliness. It might be that you've gone through a significant life change or it might have come out of nowhere. Either way, thinking about when you started to feel lonely and any potential causes is a good first step.

Have a think about:

- ♥ When you first started feeling lonely.
- ♥ What contributes to you feeling lonely.
- ♥ What helps you feel less lonely.

Jot these down and continue to add to points two and three as you notice more factors that contribute to and help ease your loneliness.

Talk it out

Loneliness might feel like a difficult or embarrassing topic to talk about but, believe me, there are people out there who want to help.

If you don't feel like you can open up to your friends or family about it, try somewhere impartial. There are lots of organisations, like the Samaritans and Mind, with people trained to listen and offer support.

Your doctor will also be able to provide guidance and signpost relevant talking therapies and options that could help you feel better.

Here are a few conversation starters that might come in handy if you're struggling to find the words.

- ♥ **To a friend:** *'Sorry I haven't been in touch lately. I've been feeling really lonely. Do you fancy catching up over a hot drink soon?'*

- ♥ **To family:** *'I love you and I'm not sure how to explain it but I've been feeling really lonely lately – I just wanted you to know.'*

- ♥ **To doctors or organisations:** *'I've been feeling really lonely and isolated lately. I'm not sure what support is out there but I'd like to discuss anything that you think could help.'*

Connect with good people

Think of loneliness in a similar way to how you think when feeling hungry. Hunger is your body's way of telling you that you need to eat. Loneliness is your mind and body's way of telling you that you need more social connection.

That's not to say that you should walk down the road starting conversations with everyone you meet. Like many things in life, it's about quality over quantity. Think about the people you enjoy spending time with and reach out to them for a coffee or catch-up. Avoid connecting with people who don't make you feel good about yourself, as this may just contribute to lonely feelings. If you need more positive people in your life, try apps like Meetup.

I know it can be really hard – especially when all you feel like doing is shutting yourself away or withdrawing – but often the most difficult part is making that first step. Once that's done, you'll feel better for it in the long run – promise.

Stop comparing yourself to others

Sometimes checking social media can make feelings of loneliness worse. If you're suffering from loneliness, try limiting your social-media time and focusing on more positive, meaningful interactions.

Because here's the thing: everyone has their own strengths and weaknesses. It's part of being human. What's plastered on Instagram is often not an accurate reflection of reality. We all struggle. We all have bad days as well as good, because none of us is perfect. Remember that.

Envying others only robs you of your own happiness. So, focus on being the best version of yourself rather than a carbon copy of anyone else.

Here are a few top tips to help you stop comparing yourself to others:

1. Detox your social media

Unfollow people who make you feel bad about yourself just by looking at their pics.

2. Focus on your achievements, not anyone else's

Comparison can undermine achievement. If someone else can do twenty press-ups and you can only do five, that doesn't make you inferior – far from it. It's still a personal achievement that you should be proud of.

3. Stop looking out, start looking in

So someone's life looks amazing? Good for them. There will always be those people whose lives seem to be shiny and perfect on the outside – but that's irrelevant to your life and success. You're on your own journey, going at your own pace. It will never be the same as anyone else's but that doesn't make it a lesser journey in any way.

Instead of investing so much time and effort into noticing the good things about others' lives, invest that time and effort into noticing the good things about yourself.

A flower does not think of the flower next to it; it just blooms.

Anonymous

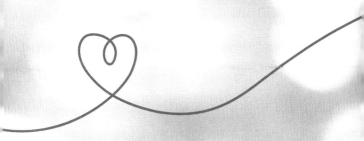

How to answer 'How are you still single?'

It's one of the most tedious questions to deal with when you're single. But don't ever let it make you question yourself or your worth. You're fabulous. Here are some kick-ass responses to have up your sleeve ready for the next time someone asks you.

Q: *Why are you still single?*
A: Because I'd rather be single and content than in an unhappy relationship, wouldn't you?

Q: *How are you still single?*
A: Because I value myself and my time too much to settle.

Q: *How are you still single?*

A: Because I'm having the best time right now. I'm focusing on my relationship with myself and it's going really well, thank you.

Q: *How are you still single?*

A: Because I don't like sharing pasta, let alone my bed, to be honest.

Q: *But you're so pretty. How are you still single?*

A: Thanks for the compliment. I am pretty – pretty damn happy on my own right now.

Q: *How is someone as smart and successful as you still single?*

A: You've kind of answered your own question there. I'm too smart to settle for a fool, and too successful to need someone else to rely on. I got this all by myself. But thanks for the compliment.

Q: *Why are you still single?*

A: Because ordinary people bore me. Tinder hurts my thumb. And I like walking around in mismatching pyjamas and no bra.

Q: *Still single?*

A: Still in a relationship/married?

Q: *How are you still single?*
A: Because I don't need a partner to prove my worth or validate my existence. I can do that all by myself.

Q: *How are you still single?*
A: Huh? I'm not. I'm in a very happy relationship with my bed and it's going really well. We can't get enough of each other – we sleep together every night.

Q: *How are you still single?*
A: Because my ex made me choose between them and the cat/dog/hair straighteners and I asked them not to slam the door on their way out.

Q: *How are you still single?*

A: Because the last person I dated wouldn't accept my pet unicorn, Your Royal Horniness, and she's my pride and joy.

Q: *Why are you still single?*

A: Because my current idea of Netflix and Chill is, quite literally, chilling in bed watching *Orange Is the New Black* back to back in a Gryffindor onesie with unlimited cups of tea.

Q: *Why are you still single?*

A: I'm not single. I'm married to pizza. We're very much in love.

Q: *Why are you still single?*

A: *Lean in and whisper* Because, underneath my clothes, I'm a Power Ranger and previous partners have struggled with my extreme fame.

THE MORAL OF
the Story

SO, REMEMBER:

1. Stop worrying if you're good enough for other people

Instead start wondering if they're good enough for you. The more you love and value yourself, the less sh*t you're willing to accept. So, know your worth and never settle for anything less. You're way too special to be taken for granted.

2. Be more selfish

Schedule in time for *you* and do more of what makes you happy. Adventure. Explore. Stay curious. Say yes more. This is your journey, so enjoy the ride.

3. Never feel you have to justify your singleness

You don't ask people to justify why they're in a relationship or married, so don't feel you have to explain yourself to anyone. Being single by choice is admirable. You're part of a generation of strong, amazingly independent singletons living their lives. Be proud.

4. Date on your terms – and only if you want to

Trust your gut. Watch out for red flags. Don't fall into the WhatsApp waiting game – you can't control when someone texts you back. And if they don't, it's their loss.

Thank you! Next…

5. You are enough. You are complete

In fact, you're a badass babe with a wonderful future!

PS I love you.

The end

(is just the beginning).

xoxo

FURTHER READING AND RESOURCES

Other great reads

- ♥ *We Should All Be Feminists* by Chimamanda Ngozi Adichie

- ♥ *Radical Acceptance: Awakening the Love That Heals Fear and Shame within Us* by Tara Brach

- ♥ *The 7 Habits of Highly Effective People: Powerful Lessons in Personal Change* by Stephen R. Covey

- ♥ *What a Time to Be Alone: The Slumflower's Guide to Why You Are Already Enough* by Chidera Eggerue

- ♥ *The Compassionate Mind: Compassion Focused Therapy* by Paul Gilbert

- ♥ *The Single Woman: Life, Love, and a Dash of Sass* by Mandy Hale

- ♥ *Self-Compassion: Stop Beating Yourself Up and Leave Insecurity Behind* by Kristin Neff

- ♥ *The Chimp Paradox: The Mind Management Programme for Confidence, Success and Happiness* by Prof Steve Peters

Awesome apps and online resources

- ♥ 10% Happier (perfect for those who want to start meditation but don't know where to begin): www.10percenthappier.com

- ♥ Down Dog (home yoga app): www.downdogapp.com

- ♥ Gratitude (app to help you find something to be grateful for every day): https://gratitude.plus

- ♥ Insight Timer (incredible meditations and mindfulness practices for free): www.insighttimer.com

- ♥ Meetup (meetups for everyone): www.meetup.com

- ♥ Stop, Breathe & Think (take a pause and enjoy great guided meditations): www.stopbreathethink.com

- ♥ The Compassionate Mind Foundation (heaps of handy self-compassion resources): www.compassionatemind.co.uk

Me date ideas

- ♥ National Trust: www.nationaltrust.org.uk
- ♥ Time Out: www.timeout.com
- ♥ Treatwell: www.treatwell.co.uk

Solo travelling inspiration

- ♥ Adventures for Solo Travelers: www.afstravelers.com
- ♥ AdventureWomen: www.adventurewomen.com
- ♥ Expedia: www.expedia.com
- ♥ Microadventures: www.alastairhumphreys.com/microadventures-3
- ♥ Rough Guides: www.roughguides.com
- ♥ Wanderlust: www.wanderlust.co.uk
- ♥ Women Traveling Together: www.women-traveling.com

Self-care must-haves

- ♥ BuddyBox (a 'hug in a box'): www.blurtitout. org/buddybox
- ♥ Dailygreatness: www.dailygreatness.co.uk
- ♥ Lower Lodge Candles (the dreamiest aromas!): www.lowerlodgecandles.com
- ♥ The Happiness Planner: thehappinessplanner. com
- ♥ The Positive Planner: www.thepositiveplanner. co.uk

People you can talk to if you're feeling lonely

- ♥ Marmalade Trust: visit marmaladetrust.org
- ♥ Mind: visit www.mind.org.uk
- ♥ Samaritans: visit www.samaritans.org
- ♥ The Blurt Foundation: www.blurtitout.org

If you're interested in finding out more about our books, find us on Facebook at **Summersdale Publishers** and follow us on Twitter at @Summersdale.

www.summersdale.com

Image credits

pp.5, 11, 14–5, 23, 26, 35, 39, 44–5, 46, 62–3, 65, 67, 72, 73, 78–9, 84–5, 88, 99, 102, 108–9, 113, 115, 122–3, 127, 132, 135, 146, 150–1, 153 – heart/pattern © vectortwins/Shutterstock.com

pp.6, 10, 17, 38, 51, 61, 69, 77, 86, 93, 105, 107, 121, 128, 136, 149 – diamond shapes © NikaMooni/Shutterstock.com

pp.18–9, 33, 36, 43, 48, 68, 81, 100, 134, 144–5 – lights © Zelenaya/Shutterstock.com

pp.21, 40, 59, 87, 117, 147 – background © Number1411/Shutterstock.com